A LOOK AT YOUR GOVERNMENT

HOW DOES A BILL BECOME A LAW?

BY KATHLEEN CONNORS

Gareth Stevens
PUBLISHING

CRASHCOURSE

Please visit our website, www.garethstevens.com. For a free color catalog of all our high-quality books, call toll free 1-800-542-2595 or fax 1-877-542-2596.

Library of Congress Cataloging-in-Publication Data

Names: Connors, Kathleen M., author.
Title: A look at your government : how does a bill become a law? / Kathleen
  Connors.
Description: New York : Gareth Stevens Publishing, [2018] | Includes index.
Identifiers: LCCN 2016027226 | ISBN 9781482460551 (pbk. book) | ISBN
  9781482460568 (6 pack) | ISBN 9781482460575 (library bound book)
Subjects: LCSH: Legislation--United States. | Law--United States--Interpretation and construc-
tion. | Statutes--Untied States. | Bill
  drafting--United States.
Classification: LCC KF4945 .C66 2018 | DDC 328.73/077--dc23
LC record available at https://lccn.loc.gov/2016027226

First Edition

Published in 2018 by
Gareth Stevens Publishing
111 East 14th Street, Suite 349
New York, NY 10003

Designer: Samantha DeMartin
Editor: Kristen Nelson

Photo credits: Series art MaxyM/Shutterstock.com; cover, pp. 1, 11, 17 (both) Chip
Somodevilla/Getty Images News/Getty Images; p. 5 (branches) Lucia Fox/Shutterstock.com;
p. 5 (buildings) JPL Designs/Shutterstock.com; p. 7 Orhan Cam/Shutterstock.com; p. 9 Barry
Blackburn/Shutterstock.com; p. 13 Rob Crandall/Shutterstock.com; p. 15 Wally McNamee/
Corbis Historical/Getty Images; p. 19 Bill Clark/CQ-Roll Call Group/Getty Images;
p. 21 (House) SAUL LOEB/AFP/Getty Images; p. 21 (Senate) Tktru/Wikimedia Commons;
p. 23 Tom Williams/CQ-Roll Call Group/Getty Images; p. 25 Pool/Getty Images News/
Getty Images; p. 27 courtesy of the Library of Congress; p. 29 (seal) Ipankonin/Wikimedia
Commons; p. 29 (Supreme Court Building) Gary Blakeley/Shutterstock.com; p. 30 (icons)
browndogstudios/Shutterstock.com; p. 30 (graph) Fireofheart/Shutterstock.com; p. 30 (bill)
kasezo/Shutterstock.com.

Printed in the United States of America

CPSIA compliance information: Batch #CS17GS: For further information contact Gareth Stevens, New York, New York at 1-800-542-2595.

CONTENTS

Words in the glossary appear in **bold** type the first time they are used in the text.

It's the Law

Everyone in the United States must follow laws. Companies and government bodies have laws governing how they work, too. Congress is the branch of the US government that makes laws. It has two houses: the Senate and the House of **Representatives**.

BRANCHES OF GOVERNMENT

LEGISLATIVE
made of up the Senate and
House of Representatives

EXECUTIVE
headed by the president;
includes heads of some
government offices

JUDICIAL
headed by the
Supreme Court;
includes lower courts

MAKE THE GRADE

The Senate has 100 members, two from each
state. The House has 435 members. The
number of representatives from each state is
based on state population.

5

BILL ON THE HILL

A law begins as a bill, or a **draft** of a law presented to Congress. Bills start as ideas presented by members of Congress. Almost all bills can start in either the Senate or the House of Representatives.

MAKE THE GRADE

Bills having to do with revenue, or money, can only start in the House of Representatives.

Each bill presented needs a sponsor, or someone to speak for it. When a member of Congress wants to sponsor a bill, he or she looks for others to cosponsor it. Having cosponsors shows **support** for the bill.

MAKE THE GRADE

Ideas for bills sometimes come from a representative or senator's **constituents**. These often have to do with making life better for these people, such as fixing roads.

CONGRESSMAN
ROB WITTMAN

9

Once a bill has some support, it's introduced to the Senate or the House of Representatives. The bill is given a number and read aloud to that house of Congress. The bill is then sent to a **committee**.

MAKE THE GRADE

To introduce a bill in the House of Representatives, a House member puts it in a special box called the hopper.

SENATOR
HARRY REID

11

In Committee

Each house of Congress has committees **focusing** on important subjects, such as farming and schools. They consider bills and deal with questions and problems on that subject. Committee members know a lot about the area of government their committee focuses on.

MAKE THE GRADE

Some committees found in both the House and Senate are those that focus on armed services, energy, and US connections with other countries.

When considering a bill, committees will hold a hearing. Committee members listen to people who support the bill and those who don't. They can make better decisions about the bill after hearing the reasoning of both sides.

MAKE THE GRADE

Most committee hearings are public. That means anyone can go and hear about bills being considered.

15

Next, committee members look at all the facts they have about the bill. They may ask for amendments, or changes, to a bill. They vote to keep changes or not. This is called a "mark-up" **session**.

MAKE THE GRADE

In mark-up sessions, changes to a bill can be small, such as changing a word or sentence. Some bills may also have a new part added or a whole part cut.

Company Discriminate
verage to Americans v
rates or dropping cover

- The nonpartisan Cong
hium costs for Americar
fectively slows the grov

ederal Deficit — Accord
er the next 10 years and
e GDP -- roughly $800 to

- Focus on Wellness an
ealth care system from
annual "wellness visit,
eficiaries, and reward

lity Health Care Cover
lity health care cover
ed care and resulting

ality This America's
ig up crooner and
ary forward assistant

t to the company state
lard. lap and course

Bingaman   219
Cornyn   Del
Stabenow   164
Crapo   274
Stabenow   hold   136
Grassley   277
Stabenow   108
Cornyn   Del   280
Wyden   hold   163
Klobuchar   55

17

DEBATE ON THE FLOOR

The bill is reported, or brought back, to the whole House or Senate after the committee agrees on what it includes and how it's written. The whole house then **debates** the bill. More amendments may be voted on.

MAKE THE GRADE

Sometimes bills are sent back to the committee. This often happens because a group wants a big change made to the bill or wants it to be tabled, or stopped altogether.

Sen. Mitch McConnell

Sen. Harry Reid

THE VOTE

In both the House and the Senate, a **majority** is needed for a bill to pass. Members of the house may vote by saying "yea" for "yes" or "nay" for "no." Or members may cast votes on a computer.

MAKE THE GRADE

A bill needs 218 of 435 votes in the House to pass. It needs 51 of 100 votes to pass in the Senate.

THE SENATE

MEMBERS OF THE HOUSE OF REPRESENTATIVES

THE NEXT HOUSE

A bill passed in one house is then sent to the other. It goes through the same steps it went through in the house where it started. Amendments and debates may change the bill again before it's voted on.

MAKE THE GRADE

A bill must pass in the same form in both houses. If the Senate makes big changes to a House bill, the House will have to vote on it again.

PRESIDENTIAL ACTIONS

A bill passed by a majority in the House and Senate goes to the president. Once the president signs it, it becomes law! However, the president can also veto it, or stop it from becoming law.

MAKE THE GRADE

Sometimes the president vetoes a bill and sends it back to Congress with notes. The bill may be changed so the president will support it.

PRESIDENT
BARACK OBAMA

25

The president can take no action on a bill, too. If Congress is in session, the bill becomes law without the president's signature after 10 days. If Congress isn't in session, after 10 days, a bill doesn't become law.

MAKE THE GRADE

When the president holds on to a bill until Congress isn't in session and doesn't sign it, it's called a pocket veto.

UNCONSTITUTIONAL

Once a bill becomes law, everyone has to follow it! But sometimes, people may think it goes against the US **Constitution**. The highest court in the land, the Supreme Court, can get rid of a law if they find that to be true.

MAKE THE GRADE

When a law goes against the Constitution, it's called unconstitutional.

SUPREME COURT
BUILDING

29

HOW A BILL BECOMES A LAW

A bill is introduced in the House or Senate.

It goes to committee.

The house votes on the bill.

If it passes, the bill goes to the other house of Congress.

The bill goes to committee again.

The house votes on the bill.

If it passes, it goes to the president.

The president signs the bill into law or vetoes it.

GLOSSARY

committee: a small group that does a certain job

constituent: someone who lives in the area represented by a member of Congress

constitution: the basic laws by which a country or state is governed

debate: to argue a side. Also, an argument or public discussion.

draft: an early form of something

focus: to have directed attention

majority: a number greater than half of the total

representative: a member of a lawmaking body who acts for voters

session: an active group meeting

support: the act of showing favor and giving help

FOR MORE INFORMATION

BOOKS

Luce, Pat, and Holly Joyner. *How a Bill Becomes a Law.* New York, NY: Scholastic, 2008.

Nelson, Robin, and Sandy Donovan. *The Congress: A Look at the Legislative Branch.* Minneapolis, MN: Lerner Publications, 2012.

WEBSITES

How Laws Are Made

kids.clerk.house.gov/grade-school/lesson.html?intID=17

Use this website to review the bill process.

Publisher's note to educators and parents: Our editors have carefully reviewed these websites to ensure that they are suitable for students. Many websites change frequently, however, and we cannot guarantee that a site's future contents will continue to meet our high standards of quality and educational value. Be advised that students should be closely supervised whenever they access the Internet.

INDEX